SLIM DOWN

Fighting Childhood Obesity with Healthy Habits

SLIM DOWN
Fighting Childhood Obesity with Healthy Habits

Pierpaolo R. Palmieri, M.D., F.A.A.P.

Universal Publishers/uPUBLISH.com
USA · 2000

Slim Down:
Fighting Childhood Obesity with Healthy Habits

Universal Publishers/uPUBLISH.com
USA · 2000

ISBN: 1-58112-744-8

www.upublish.com/books/ palmieri.htm

For Emma, Stefano, and Sabrina.

Outline

Part I: The Problem of Childhood Obesity

1. An American Epidemic

The reasons for the recent increase in obesity in the United States are reviewed. The health complications related to obesity are discussed.

2. Energy Balance: How The Body Works

Weight gain is always due to taking in more calories, in the form of food, than are expended through work and exercise. Useful terms such as calorie, Basal Metabolic Rate (BMR), Thermogenic Effect of Food (TEF), and Total Energy Expenditure (TEE) are introduced and defined.

3. Is my child overweight? Gland Problems and Other Myths

Definitions of obesity and overweight for adults are introduced, as is the concept of Body Mass Index (BMI). The normal growth pattern for children is reviewed. In childhood, obesity is best defined by a pattern of weight gain that does not coincide with what is expected for that age, utilizing gender appropriate growth curves.

4. **Setting the right goals for each child- one size does NOT fit all**

Due to continued growth in children, weight loss is not necessary for many children. Rather, a decline in the rate of weight gain is sufficient in most cases. Most importantly, the goal should not be a predetermined target weight, but the incorporation of healthy habits which we hope the child will engage in throughout his life. Weight is de-emphasized; health is stressed.

Part II: The Solution

5. **S = Sit at the table to eat: No More Moveable Feasts!**

Children tend to overeat if they eat in the car, while doing homework, and especially, in front of the television. Having the child sit at the table to eat helps him be more aware of signals of hunger and satiety and prevents overeating.

6. **L = Limit television viewing : No More Flabby Bodies or Flabby Minds!**

The amount of time a child spends watching television has been found to be one of the most important predictors of obesity in childhood.

7. **I = Include exercise as an essential activity of daily living: Moving is a Pleasure, Not a Chore!**

Exercise is essential to maintain health and fitness in our society due to all the luxuries we are afforded which reduce the physical activity necessary to earn a living. Not only do we burn calories by exercising; we also increase our lean body mass. This allows us to continue burning calories at a higher rate even when we are at rest. No weight management program can be successful if it does not incorporate regular exercise.

8. **M = Motivate your child with rewards: Payoffs will Pay Off!**

The methods of behavioral modification are summarized. Positive reinforcement, rather than punishment, should be adopted as the method for changing childhood behaviors.

9. **D = Dine restaurant style not buffet style: Portion Control Leads to Appetite Control!**

An approach to meals which reduces the likelihood of eating seconds and overeating is introduced.

10. O = Offer fewer, better snacks: Learn to Love Those Veggies!

By eliminating high fat, calorically dense, between-meal snacks a significant number of calories can be eliminated over a long period of time. Only low-fat snacks, of nutritiously sensible foods such as fresh fruits and raw vegetables, should be offered as snacks to children.

11. W = When in doubt, walk: Hidden Opportunities to Burn Calories!

Extra calories can be burned by taking the stairs rather than riding an elevator, walking to the store rather than driving (when safe and practical), and by doing chores and housework. All of these activities can be done in a fun way.

12. N = Never talk the talk if you can't walk the walk: Be a Role Model, Not a Dictator!

One cannot expect a child to perform behaviors and incorporate habits which are foreign to his parents. The importance of parents serving as role models is emphasized.

TABLE OF CONTENTS

Part I

The Problem

Chapter 1

An Epidemic

The last decade of the twentieth century served as the setting for an epidemic in the United States which will have long-lasting public health repercussions. An infectious agent was not responsible for this epidemic, and so physicians could not prevent its further spread. Despite many advances in the understanding of this condition, especially in the field of molecular genetics, there is no immunization or other medicinal cure in sight.

This condition is associated with many serious illnesses, which constitute the most frequent reasons for physician visits by adults. Among these are heart disease, high blood pressure, elevated cholesterol levels, diabetes, orthopedic problems, gallbladder disease, and even certain forms of cancer. As a result, individuals afflicted with this condition have a higher risk of premature death than the rest of the population. Sadly, children who are delivered by women with this condition are more likely to be born with birth defects such as spina bifida (where the spinal column does not finish developing, often resulting in paralysis of the legs), and anencephaly (where most or all of the brain is missing).

Alarmingly, more than one third of U.S. children now have this condition, considerably more than the proportion affected twenty years ago, and so we are now witnessing a surge in the frequency of complications of this condition at younger ages. A notable example is adult onset (or Type II) diabetes, which has significantly increased in frequency in the teenage population in recent years.

The condition I am referring to is, of course, obesity. It is estimated that in this country approximately 65% of men and 55% of women aged 25 or older are overweight or obese. About 300,000 deaths per year can be directly attributed to obesity in this country, which is nearly identical to the total number of people who succumbed to AIDS in the United States through 1999.

From the amount of money spent on treating obesity in adults, including designer diets, exercise programs, medications, and surgery, and considering the meager results obtained from most of these methods, it is clear that the most effective approach in the battle of the bulge is prevention. Because the development of obesity is increasing among children, the prevention effort must clearly start in childhood.

There is another compelling reason to address this issue early in life. Basically, old dogs have a hard time learning new tricks. Typically, we form most of our habits by the end of the teenage years. For example, it is uncommon for someone to become addicted to cigarettes if one does not start smoking before the age of eighteen. Most chronic smokers started early in life. The earlier you start, the harder it is to kick the habit.

There is no doubt that the most effective approach to combating obesity is adopting changes that include regular exercise, avoidance of a sedentary lifestyle, and the consumption of a balanced diet without an excessive number of calories. This fact is hard for many to accept, because results do not come quickly, and it requires sustained effort for a long period of time -your entire life. There are dozens of weight loss programs that promise quick, effortless results. Some programs actually promise weight loss without exercise while allowing the consumption of more food! Many programs utilize vitamins, minerals and herbs, suggesting the preposterous notion that obesity is due to a nutritional deficiency. A few claim that eating the right combination of foods will achieve weight loss. Of course the medical community contributes to the confusion of the public by prescribing appetite suppressants, as if the reason for obesity was just a matter of too much hunger.

There are basically two explanations for the popularity of weight loss programs based on illogical or absolutely ridiculous principles. One is the lack of scientific sophistication typical of the average American. Some people mistrust the method of study and analysis that has contributed the most to man's understanding of how nature works. I know of no newspaper in the country that doesn't have an astrology section. You don't read the newspaper? No problem. You can dial a 1-900 number and consult a psychic by telephone. Why this remarkable individual who is able to foretell the future is waiting for your call to charge you by the minute instead of earning millions with the stock market remains a mystery.

The other reason for the success of these programs is the deep sense of despair and helplessness that many have when it comes to managing their weight. It is often the most desperate who are likely to fall for such schemes, as they have the greatest desire and need to believe in them. The fact remains that "lose pounds fast" programs are as likely to work as "get rich quick" schemes. When the weight loss program fails, as it inevitably does, the individual's feeling of helplessness grows, the hope for successful weight control fades and the individual believes, "Nothing works, I've tried everything". The truth is they've only tried the wrong things.

The SLIM DOWN approach is not a "lose all your weight quickly and effortlessly" scheme. It is a blueprint for a healthy lifestyle. The focus is not on weight or pounds, but on behavior. Adopting these desirable behaviors leads to improved fitness and health, which is the ultimate goal, rather than shooting for a target weight. The aim is to acquaint children with a life-style of regular exercise, avoidance of inactivity, and maintaining a healthy relationship with food. The goal is for children to incorporate these life-style changes into their daily routine, and utilize them every day: not just during their childhood years, but into adulthood.

The reasons for weight control are many. The health benefits are primary, but equally important is how enhanced physical appearance increases one's feelings of self-worth. A person who is very overweight is often regarded as having poor impulse control or is judged to be generally lazy. Obesity can have a negative impact on job promotion and employment. Our appearance is not just a cosmetic issue, whether it is the manner in which we dress, walk, and talk, our hairstyle, or whether or not we have tattoos or wear jewelry on our nose. It communicates to others how we view ourselves, our values, and who we aim to be.

Finally, one can invoke a spiritual explanation for wanting to maintain a healthy weight. If we believe that our life is a gift granted to us by a creator, not by mere chance, but perhaps to serve a specific purpose, we then realize that we have a duty to preserve our health in order to fulfill our mission. We cannot show a lack of appreciation for the opportunity given to us, by destroying our body with drugs, alcohol, or by not maintaining fitness. The body is our temple. We must not vandalize or desecrate it.

Chapter 2

Energy Balance

The regulation of body weight is ultimately a phenomenon of energy balance. If the input of energy into the body exceeds the output, the body gains weight. If the output exceeds the input, the body loses weight. Energy is put into the body by eating food. Energy is taken out of the body through physical exertion.

The energy of food is contained in the chemical bonds between the different atoms that make up the food molecules. Cleaving these bonds can release energy in the form of heat, which is measured in calories. A calorie is the amount of heat required to raise the temperature of one gram of water by one degree centigrade. In nutrition, energy is more easily measured in kilocalories (kcal) or Calories (with a capital c). A kilocalorie is 100 calories, or if you prefer, the amount of heat required to raise the temperature of one kilogram of water by one degree centigrade.

The universe behaves according to laws of physics, which unlike laws created by man cannot be broken, even if no one is looking. Heat transfer is governed by the laws of thermodynamics, which state that in a closed system energy can neither be created nor destroyed - the sum total of energy remains the same. Thus, once heat energy is inserted into a human body in the form of food, the energy cannot just disappear or dissolve. The body, by performing work, can consume the energy, but whatever is left over will be stored. Unfortunately, the most efficient storage form that our bodies have for energy is fat, not muscle. If it were otherwise we could all eat our way to looking like Arnold Schwarzenegger.

Therefore, if an individual takes in more energy than he needs for the amount of work his body performs, he will gradually increase the amount of fat composition of his body. Note that the absolute amount of food taken in is not as important as the balance between energy input and output. So it is entirely possible to eat relatively little, but still gain weight, if one has an extremely sedentary lifestyle.

Let's take the example of an imaginary credit card that charges no interest (yes, it's too good to be true). I use the card and the first month charge $60. At the end of the month I pay just the minimum payment due of $10. The balance is $50. The second month I charge another $60 and pay the minimum payment of $15. The balance is now $95. It is easy to see that if I continue at this slow, steady rate, within a year or two I will be severely in debt.

This is precisely what happens with many people who gradually, over a long period of time, incur a huge caloric debt. They often wonder how they could have accumulated so much weight. After all, they don't eat that much. And perhaps, they do exercise a little. "It must be my metabolism", they conclude. The basic, undeniable truth is that they ate too much for the amount of exercise they did, or if you prefer, they didn't exercise enough for the quantity of food they ate. Just be thankful our body doesn't charge us interest every month!

Just yesterday I read a story in the newspaper about an 840 pound woman in Philadelphia who required the assistance of the fire department to lift her out of her second-story window with a crane in order to take her to a hospital. She had sustained some minor injuries when she fell as she attempted to get out of bed. The paramedics and firefighters were unable to carry her down the stairs and out the front door due to her large size. The woman, who was in her fifties, hadn't left her home in three years. I read recently as well about an 800 pound man in California who required similar assistance leaving his house to go to the hospital.

I wonder what these people were like when they were children? Certainly they did not aspire to become morbidly obese. Like all children, they must have had dreams and hopes for the future. I doubt that either one woke up one morning and just decided to become fat. If I had to speculate on how they arrived at the point of morbid obesity, I would guess that they probably started having a weight problem at a relatively early age. Perhaps as a result of the weight, they became increasingly frustrated with interpersonal relationships, but were able to find solace and relief in eating.

At some point, the idea of having interaction with people may have became too painful due to their constant staring and hushed comments about size. One can reach a stage where one feels there is no point in trying to continue fighting. In behavioral psychology this is sometimes described as "learned helplessness". Thus, these people may have taken refuge in their homes, where they did not have to be seen by anyone except the people closest to them, and continued indulging in the pleasure of food, to numb the pain caused by the realization that true happiness was nowhere in reach. If you weigh 500 pounds it doesn't really matter if you gain another 100 pounds, so why try to change?

It is actually remarkable how closely energy input and output is regulated for the majority of adults. For most adults, body weight tends to remain quite stable over long periods of time despite occasional short-term fluctuations in eating and exercise patterns. In my hands I have an average size (2.3 ounces to be exact) milk chocolate crunch bar. It contains 330 Calories. If I were to eat one of these chocolate bars twice a week, and were able to maintain the rest of my diet and the amount of exercise I do unchanged, in one year I would incur a debt of 34,320 Calories. Since 3,500 Calories is equivalent to one pound of body fat, I would gain almost 10 pounds.

It is unlikely that this would actually happen to me because my body would do something to compensate for the increase in caloric intake. For example, those chocolate bars might affect my appetite later in the day so that I would eat less of other foods. Or I may consciously compensate by exercising more. The point is that you don't have to be a glutton to become fat. The flip side is that if an individual were able to just eliminate one chocolate bar a week from his diet and do nothing else, he would lose almost five pounds in a year. I did warn you that I am not offering a get slim quick plan, didn't I?

Useful Energy Concepts

The obesity prevention and treatment program I am proposing in this book will not require the calculation of calories ingested or consumed, or the weighing of every portion of food prepared. Only the most compulsive individuals would be able to maintain such a regimen over a significant period of time. Nor will I recommend a specific diet for breakfast, lunch and dinner. I am proud of the fact that I will not waste precious paper and ink on the almost obligatory list of recipes (which no one ever uses) found in almost every "diet" book. If you really want some recipes you can buy a cookbook (might I suggest Italian cuisine?).

However, I do want to go over some numbers and terminology so that you may see that the methods I will advise you to employ are scientifically and mathematically sound, and that the approach as a whole is logical. This will help to convince you that my complete approach to obesity prevention does work because it works in accordance to physical laws, which as you already know, cannot be broken, even if you have a good lawyer.

More on Calories

We already went over the definition of a calorie. Be aware that a calorie is a calorie, regardless of whether the source is carbohydrate (starches and sugars), protein, or fat. There is no such thing as a "fattening food". Any and all foods will make you fat if you eat enough of them. That is why millions of people spend billions of dollars on "diet" foods and drinks and still gain weight.

While in college I worked at a family -run Italian restaurant. The food was excellent and served in generous portions. One of our regular customers was an extremely obese woman. She would routinely order the chicken Cacciatore, which was half of a large chicken cooked in a sauce with mushrooms and bell peppers. The dinner included soup (minestrone) and salad, a side dish of pasta with either meat or marinara sauce, and a slice of homemade ricotta cheesecake.

She was a good eater. Her parents would have been proud. One might say she had a "healthy" appetite. It seems she never met a meal she did not like. Her plate would always be clean at the end of the dinner. But of course she did drink diet cola (she even brought her own can) and would only use Sweet and Low in her coffee. Perhaps she thought that if only she could consume more diet cola and Sweet and Low she would one day become thin. Or maybe, that the diet drinks could somehow eliminate the calories ingested, like a nutritional black hole.

There are many slim people who eat so-called "fattening foods", and don't gain weight. That is seen by some as proof that some people just don't gain weight, no matter what. The world is so unfair! What they fail to look at is the sum-total of the slim person's energy intake and output – the totality of the individual's dietary and exercise habits.

So for now, let's say that strictly speaking, it doesn't necessarily matter what you eat. What matters is the total amount of calories ingested. It is true that some foods contain more calories than others do. A gram of fat contains 9 kilocalories, whereas a gram of protein or carbohydrate contains 4 kilocalories. Thus, it does make sense to try to diminish the percentage of fat in the diet. Also, there is no question that a serving of fruit is nutritionally superior to a serving of potato chips.

Traditional nutritional advice suggests that for adults, 10 to 15% of the caloric intake should come from protein, less than 35% should come from fat, and the rest from carbohydrates. What are the exact proportions in my diet? How should I know? I don't sit down at meals with a food analyzer, a scale and a scientific calculator to compute my energy intake. Nor do I want to follow a strict pre-determined diet, where the calories are already calculated out for me. Some days I feel like eating pasta, but there are times that I crave a hamburger. Most people can relate to this.

Again, I will not bore you with scores of recipes you will never use. At this point suffice it to say that a diet that consists of fruits and vegetables, including pasta, rice and bread as staples, along with only moderate amounts of lean meat is probably going to have an appropriately low percentage of calories originating from dietary fat. In cases of extreme obesity, I do recommend a formal consultation with a nutritionist in order to evaluate the diet and see if it can be improved.

Energy Expenditure

Energy input is in the form of food. The total energy output by the body is known as Total Energy Expenditure (TEE) and is composed of Basal Metabolic Rate (BMR), Thermogenic (or Thermic) Effect of Food (TEF), and physical activity (PA).

BMR

The basal or resting metabolic rate, which is expressed in terms of calories per unit of time, is the amount of energy consumed by an individual at rest, in a state of satiety, at a comfortable ambient temperature. It is the energy consumed by the body when it is idling, to carry out vital functions such as breathing and pumping of the heart. It is, more or less, the level of energy consumption your child is at when he is laying down on the couch, zoned out in front of the television. BMR accounts for roughly 60 to 75% of Total Energy Expenditure, but can vary widely between individuals based on the amount of physical activity performed and their body composition. For example, a bicycle racer at the Tour de France will have a smaller percentage of his Total Energy Expenditure coming from his BMR because so much of it will be due to physical activity.

Even at rest, lean tissue such as muscle consumes more energy than fat tissue. Obese adults have a higher BMR than their slim counterparts, mainly because they have more tissue to support, but when BMR is expressed per unit of body weight, obese people end up having a relatively lower BMR.

In children this association is not yet established. Children of obese parents, who are at greater risk of developing obesity, have been found to have relatively low BMRs when compared to their peers. Nevertheless, large cross-sectional studies have shown that children and adolescents who were already obese had similar or higher levels of BMR when compared to age-matched slim children when expressed in terms of their body weight. Therefore, in children it appears that obesity is not related to relatively lower basal metabolic rates.

Thermogenic Effect of Food (TEF)

After eating a meal, energy consumption increases above the basal metabolic rate. In essence, after eating, our bodies rev at a higher RPM. This is known as the Thermogenic Effect of Food. About 10% of the energy ingested as food is lost as heat when eating a balanced diet.

There are some diet plans which suggest eating frequent meals or certain foods to boost the TEF. This approach makes little sense. There are no foods that stimulate your metabolic rate so that you burn more calories. The number of calories that you take in with the food is always much larger than the number of calories that is burned by digesting, absorbing and processing those nutrients. Thus, when you eat there is always a net intake of calories.

This logic is reminiscent of someone who spends and spends because all the items he is buying are on sale. He may boast of how much money he has saved, but actually the net flow of money was out of his wallet and into the store's cash register, not the other way around. If he really had wanted to save money, he would have bought nothing.

Physical Activity

The amount of calories burned with physical activity can vary tremendously among different individuals. On average, physical activity accounts for about 20% of the Total Energy Expenditure. In very active individuals, however, it can account for 40 to 60%. It is important to note that of all the different forms of energy expenditure, physical activity is the only one over which we have conscious control. We don't have control over the thermogenic effect of food, nor can we reset our BMR at a higher level like a thermostat. But we do have complete control over the amount of calories we burn with physical activity.

The number of calories burned for different forms of exercise for an individual weighing 150 pounds are listed in Table 1. Be aware that the actual number of calories burned can vary significantly for different individuals. For any given activity, an aerobically unfit or obese person will burn more calories than an aerobically fit, slim individual. Also, this table only takes into account the number of calories burned while performing the activity itself. It does not include the number of calories that continue to be burned when the activity is finished.

After a period of exercise, the body continues to burn calories at a higher rate for up to several hours, as it undertakes processes to restore homeostasis, or steady-state conditions. In other words, post-exercise energy expenditure is higher than pre-exercise energy expenditure. Furthermore, if exercise is maintained over a long period of time, this will result in an increase in lean body mass by increasing muscle mass and decreasing fat stores. As you already know, muscle burns more calories than fat at rest.

Thus, physical activity results in:

1. an immediate caloric expenditure during the activity itself
2. a short-term post-exercise energy expenditure for several hours after the activity is complete, and
3. a long-term increase in resting metabolic rate by increasing lean body mass.

Key Points:

Energy cannot be created nor destroyed in a closed system. Therefore, whatever energy enters your body in the form of food will either be consumed by performing work, or will remain stored in your body in the form of fat. All food can make you fat if you eat enough of it. It is very easy to build up a caloric debt and there is no way to declare bankruptcy and start again with a clean slate.

When it comes to energy regulation, there are only two variables that we have conscious control over: the amount of energy we put into our body in the form of food, and the amount that we burn in the form of physical activity. It doesn't take a rocket scientist to figure out that these are the two variables we will need to work with to achieve success in controlling weight.

Table 1

Number of Calories Burned in 30 Minutes for Different Forms of Activity
(For an individual weighing 150 pounds)

Sitting down	45
Standing quietly	50
Mopping floor	120
Bicycling at 5.5 miles per hour	135
Walking at 4 miles per hour	160
Dancing	200
Tennis	220
Running at 11.5 minutes per mile	275
Basketball	280
Cross country skiing	290

Chapter 3

Is My Child Overweight? Does He Have a Glandular Problem?

To determine if a person is overweight, we naturally look at how many pounds they weigh. But that is not enough, since we would expect a tall individual to weigh more than a short one. Therefore, doctors use a measure called the Body Mass Index (BMI) to determine if someone is truly overweight.

The BMI is calculated by dividing a person's weight in kilograms, by the square of that person's height in meters. For teenagers and adults, overweight is defined by a BMI of 25 or higher. Obesity is defined by a BMI of 30 or higher.

In younger children BMI is less useful, so we refer to standardized growth charts. If a child lies above the curve corresponding to the 95th percentile for his age, he is overweight. In most cases one can make a pretty accurate guess as to whether a child is overweight even without using fancy charts or calculations. In the my medical office, if I see a four year old boy who has a bigger beer-belly than his father, or looks about 7 months pregnant, I know he is obese before plotting him on a chart. Although dimples on the face are completely normal and actually even cute, when they are all over a child's abdomen, they are neither.

If you truly are unsure as to whether your child's weight is within the normal range you can ask your pediatrician to show you your child's growth chart. When you do so, don't look just at the weight, but also at the height. The vast majority of children I see who are overweight are taller than average for their age. This is basically a testament to the fact that they are over-nourished.

A parent sometimes asks me if I think that the child's obesity is due to a "gland" problem. In almost all cases I can answer that question without obtaining thyroid function tests or other laboratory studies. There are some rare medical problems which have obesity as one accompanying sign. In virtually all of these syndromes, the children tend to be short, developmentally delayed or have other accompanying physical manifestations. Examples of these syndromes are Prader Willi syndrome, Down syndrome, Laron dwarfism, Cushing's disease, and hypothyroidism. Some medications can also cause weight gain, most notably long-term use of steroids which are used to treat a variety of chronic childhood illnesses.

If you're child is overweight, but on the tall side, is doing all right in school, and has an otherwise normal physical exam it is highly unlikely that he has a medical problem as a cause of his obesity.

It is useful for parents to understand the normal growth pattern of children through different ages. The first year of life is characterized by the fastest growth rate of any other period in life. An infant will typically double his birth weight by four months of age, and more than triple his birth weight by one year of age. That's why infants in the first few months of life are never picky eaters, and insist on being fed every three to four hours (more frequently for breast-fed babies).

Somewhere between ten and fifteen months of age however, the rate of growth starts to slow down, and children start being a little more picky about what they eat. They're not hungry all the time anymore. Between one and five years of age, children go through a period of distinctly slow growth. During this time children typically only gain between four and a half, to five pounds a year. There may be no weight gain at all over a one or two month period. Compare that to a baby who weighed seven pounds at birth and gained a full seven pounds in his first four months of life.

A normal nine month old baby tends to be rather chubby like the Michelin tire man. But after his first birthday he should become progressively more slender. By five years of age he should be quite slim, and you'll probably be able to faintly see his lower ribs. This is the normal progression. A two-year old child who is continuing to gain weight at the same rate as a two-month old is not growing normally.

Therefore, I don't make any effort to control the rate of weight gain in the first year of life. It is not until after one year of age that I universally recommend instituting healthy habits and a healthy attitude towards food and eating.

Chapter 4

Setting the Right Goals

Before we start a trip, we must be sure we know where we plan to go. The SLIM DOWN program is the road map. Let's be clear on our destination.

From time to time I hear friends and acquaintances say that they need to lose about five or ten pounds. They usually set a timeline or a deadline. "I need to lose about eight pounds. I think I can do it in three weeks."

Or if they're quite committed to trying to lose weight they might just complain, "If I weighed ten pounds less I'd be in pretty good shape". This last statement is completely false. If you lose a few pounds by using laxatives, diuretics and dehydrating yourself you are certainly not any healthier. You are only in better shape if you become more active, exercise regularly, and eat a balanced diet which contains only a moderate amount of fat. If merely weighing less were the ultimate goal, you could just chop off a leg and weigh less.

Achieving a target weight should not be the goal. Weight is overemphasized in weight loss programs. The way I approach this is by viewing weight as only one piece of information, a physical sign which reveals that there is an underlying problem. The weight is not the disease; it is only a symptom. The problem is the lifestyle. The weight is only useful in that it brings attention to the underlying problem and allows us to address it.

As an analogy, let's take the example of a child who comes to the Emergency Room because of vomiting. The evaluation reveals that the child has appendicitis. Now, we wouldn't just administer an anti-emetic for the vomiting and send the child home. The vomiting is not going to be the main focus of our treatment of this patient. It was only significant in that it brought attention to the underlying problem. The doctors must now concentrate on the appendicitis, and not be satisfied if the child seems to be throwing up less frequently.

The relentless obsession around weight that many people have is likewise misguided. Yes, if you are overweight that should make you aware that your lifestyle needs some adjustment, but the focus should be on the lifestyle, not the weight. If you happened to lose two pounds, but you are not exercising and leading a basically sedentary lifestyle, you are no better off.

The goal of this program is to achieve health, not a target weight. The focus is on behavior and lifestyle changes, not a number on a scale. The ultimate goal is to help your children incorporate healthy habits that they will use throughout their lives. These healthy habits include exercise on a regular basis, avoiding a sedentary, inactive lifestyle, developing a healthy attitude toward eating, and consuming a balanced diet with only a moderate amount of dietary fat.

I do not expect a child to go on a diet to lose a certain number of pounds over a certain number of weeks. I am not requesting an effort lasting a few months. I encourage effort over an entire lifetime. My hope is that children get used to exercise as an essential part of their lives, and will continue to exercise when they are eighteen, twenty-five, forty-two, seventy-five, until their very last day on this planet.

The focus is on behavior. Do the right things and health will follow. The weight will take care of itself.

If one absolutely needs the feedback and reassurance of a number on a scale, I recommend checking the weight infrequently: only once every month or two should do. Just like an investor who is in the stock market for the long haul rather than short-term speculation doesn't need to check on his stocks' performance every day, you should not check your weight every day. The gain or loss of a pound here and there has little meaning in the long run.

For most children before the teenage years, the good news is that they don't need to lose any weight. Since they are still growing, slowing down the rate of weight gain is a sign that they are becoming fit. Rather than gaining ten pounds over a period of six months, we may observe that they are only gaining one or two pounds. That is real progress.

For teenagers who are very overweight, for whom we'd expect weight loss to result from adopting the healthy habits I describe in the book, I would be very encouraged initially by weight stabilization. You have to learn how to walk before you learn how to run. An obese teenager who has not lost any weight over the first six months of adopting his new lifestyle, but has also not gained any additional weight is doing very well. This should be interpreted as success, not defeat. Over the next six months, if the child continues with the program, weight loss is sure to follow.

There is only one rule for undertaking this program, which is to make it a family effort. The suggestions that I make in this book can only be successful if adopted by the entire family. If not, the child with the weight problem will feel like everyone else is picking on him or her. Every member of the household should adopt every behavior that is expected of the child.

Good health is the ultimate goal. Healthy habits over an entire lifetime are the method of achieving the goals. Weight and cosmetic issues are only secondary considerations. If you do the right things, reaching a healthy weight will follow.

Part II

The Solution

Chapter 5

S = Sit at the Table When You Eat

Walk up to the concession counter of any movie theater in the country and you will see the usual display of popcorn serving sizes, ranging from the size of your typical air-sickness bag to that of a small Jacuzzi tub. Why do theatres offer such large bounties of popcorn to moviegoers? It's because they are well aware that people who are distracted can eat much larger quantities of food than those who are paying attention to the act of eating.

Most people have had the experience of taking a few handfuls of popcorn before the movie starts, truly savoring those first few bites. Then the previews start rolling and eventually you become completely enthralled by the movie. By this time the hand and the mouth are on automatic pilot. The hand slowly reaches into the bucket, brings a scoop of kernels to the mouth where they are slowly chewed without any conscious effort. Eventually, the hand reaches down into the bucket and to your complete surprise, the bucket is empty.

This form of "unconscious" eating takes place not just in movie theaters, but in all kinds of other settings. People eat in their cars, while walking around in shopping malls, seated at a desk while doing homework, and while watching television.

Children who are allowed to eat whenever and wherever they want simply eat more. They tend to eat junk (it's hard to eat a salad while window-shopping, although there are a few courageous souls who give it a try). As a result of our busy society's desire to multi-task stuff while eating, we have developed a cuisine that requires no forks, spoons, or knives: everything is either in a sandwich or on a stick.

People who eat only while seated at the table, and who are   not engaged in other simultaneous activities (such as reading the newspaper or watching TV) are less likely to overeat. This is especially true for children, who get bored after a little while, ask to be excused from the table and want to move on to something else.

When we're not distracted during a meal we also tend to pay closer attention to our bodies' signals of hunger and satiety. Pay attention to what your body is telling you. Before starting a meal we should be aware of a feeling of hunger which is truly very difficult to describe. It is an uncomfortable (but typically not painful) feeling from the throat, down to the abdomen.

The feeling of hunger peaks when we see or smell food, at which time the experience includes an increase in salivation. With the first few bites the overwhelming sensation of hunger starts to abate. Gradually, as we continue to eat, the true physical perception of hunger disappears altogether but we may keep eating for a variety of psychological and social reasons.

If we keep eating, our general sensation shifts from one of pleasant satisfaction to a feeling of fullness, tightness and tension in the abdomen, and generalized mild discomfort. These body cues should not be misinterpreted as "Gee, I had a great meal".

In reality the body is trying to tell us "You ate too much!" It is important to pay attention to the messages our bodies are sending us, but that is hard to do if we're busy watching the season finale of "Ally McBeal".

Sometimes we eat even though we are aware that we're not really hungry. If people ate only when they were hungry and stopped as soon as the sensation of hunger was gone there would be a lot fewer overweight individuals. Unfortunately, many people are raised to believe that they cannot really trust their appetite in regulating the timing and amount of food to eat. There are many reasons people eat even when they're not hungry. Here are some pretty common ones:

- **Opportunistic**: Aunt Lucy is in town and, well, no one can beat her lasagna. Who knows when I'll have another chance to eat it!

- **Economic**: I paid $9.99 for this buffet. I'd better get my money's worth.

- **Cosmetic**: Boy, that sure looks good. I'll just have a bite.

- **Humanitarian**: We mustn't waste any food. There are children starving in Africa.
- **Covert**: Mom put a lot of effort into preparing this meal. I'd better not tell her I already ate a burger on the way home.
- **Punctual**: It's noon. Time for me to eat!
- **Medical**: If I don't eat I might get sick.
- **Celebratory**: It's Thanksgiving!

A common reason for overeating is a lack of fulfilling, meaningful personal relationships in one's life. One tries to erase the loneliness, frustration and emptiness inside by attempting to establish a fulfilling relationship with food. At the end of an eating binge, however, the stomach may be full, but the person will not be emotionally fulfilled. More common feelings are guilt and self-loathing.

It is essential to teach children that they should eat only when seated at the dinner table. If a child is sitting in front of the television and starts feeling hungry he can either wait for the program to finish and then head to the table for a snack, or he can shut the TV off, eat, and then return to the television. Eating in front of the television will predictably lead to overeating.

Have every member of your family sit down at the table to eat. Keep the television out of the dining room, and keep the dinner table out of the television room. And don't eat in the car. You'll not only improve your eating habits; you'll also save the upholstery.

Chapter 6

L = Limit Television Viewing

The American Academy of Pediatrics has recently launched a campaign addressing children's television viewing habits. Although the Academy (of which I am a fellow - that is, I finally decided to pay the annual membership fee) is mainly worried about exposing your children to inappropriate programs which might have a negative impact on their psychological and emotional development, my major concern is that television makes you fat.

The typical school age child spends most of his day in school seated at a desk. Unfortunately, fewer children are participating in regular physical education classes than a generation ago, so most kids are basically sedentary throughout the school day. When they return home they must sit around some more to finish their homework. They don't walk five miles each way to and from school in the snow, uphill both ways, the way you and I did!

If after finishing their assigned homework, they park in front of the television set for three hours until dinner is ready, they are truly leading a sedentary lifestyle. It should not be surprising that there is a direct correlation between the number of hours a child watches television per day and his risk for obesity. Some studies, in fact, suggest that the amount of television viewing is the single greatest predictive factor for obesity in childhood.

Not only does television viewing encourage a sedentary lifestyle, it also promotes the consumption of snacks which are high in fat and calories. Watch any program intended for younger audiences and you will see that the advertisements are almost exclusively for toys and junk food. Recently the character of Joe Camel was attacked because it directly marketed an unhealthy product-cigarettes-to children.

I predict that in the near future a whole parade of new suspects will go the way of Joe Camel for peddling their own unhealthy products. After all, seventy percent of the attorneys in the world practice in the United States. They have to keep busy somehow. Fortunately for them, it seems that common sense and the legal process in America divorced each other long ago, and there is no sign of reconciliation in sight. Likely to be included in the coming purge are Ronald McDonald, the Pillsbury Doughboy, Chester the Cheetah, and the cute little M&M characters (they'll have a heck of a time devising a way to keep them behind bars). The Taco Bell Chihuahua will escape conviction only after the intervention of animal rights activists.

The other thing you may notice if you watch children's programs or, for that matter, many adult programs, as well as music videos, is how quickly everything moves. Rarely does the camera stay fixed on a single subject for more than a couple of seconds at a time. The scenery is constantly shifting. Is it any surprise that more than ever children are having difficulty focusing their attention and staying on task at school? I believe that television is contributing to the epidemic of hyperactivity and attention deficit disorder we are witnessing in this country by habituating children's brains to function at hyper-speed.

Of course there are some programs that manage to educate as well as entertain. That's why

I recommend limiting television to a maximum of ninety minutes per day rather than eliminating it altogether. The key to almost everything in life is moderation. The only exception to the ninety-minute rule is if your child is watching a sporting event. In this case it is allowable to surpass the hour and a half mark in order to take advantage of what I call the Wimbledon effect.

Tennis players are aware that it is harder to find an open court during and after the Wimbledon tournament than at any other time of the year. The reason for this is that when you watch a sporting event on TV you are often compelled to go out and mimic your favorite star. This can be an especially powerful force for children who often idolize professional players. In this case, watching television can actually promote an increase in physical activity.

The question is, "How do you pry a child away from the TV set?" In practice you cannot just walk up to your child, tell him that you want him to watch less television and expect immediate compliance. In order to limit the amount of time your child spends in front of the television you must provide satisfying alternatives. This requires active involvement on your part. For example, you can go for a walk in the park with your child, ride bikes together, throw the baseball around in the backyard, read a book together, or get involved in a hobby which both of you enjoy, such as building model airplanes.

Again, it is not enough to just tell your child to "read a book or something". Active participation on the part of the parent is essential. This requires the investment of time. Children need and demand your time, your presence, and your active involvement in their lives. Time (I'm talking "quantity time", not the very convenient, no-guilt-involved "quality time") is the most valuable investment you can make towards your child's wellbeing.

Of course prevention is the preferred approach. Avoid having your child watch television in the first year of life. Thereafter, make sure you are using the television for entertainment and education rather than as a cheap babysitter. Don't let your toddlers become addicted to TV.

Television is no longer the only technology which contributes to obesity. Video games and computers also can trap your child in a sedentary life-style. While these activities may have value-the development of motor skills, reading skills, exposure to new ideas and new ways of learning-an increased risk of obesity is one of the prices society pays for progress.

Chapter 7

I = Include Exercise as an Essential Activity of Daily Living

There are many activities which we perform as a routine on a daily basis. Some of these are basic to our survival and are effortless, carried out without much mental planning, such as breathing, eating, going to the bathroom, and sleeping. Whether or not you are effective at organizing your time you will carry out all these tasks within the next twenty-four hours.

There are other activities we engage in either to comply with social norms or to avoid negative consequences. These include bathing, brushing our teeth, clipping our toenails and shaving various parts of our bodies depending on our gender and state of mental health.

Despite the hectic pace of life that many of us are engaged in, almost everyone somehow manages to sleep, eat, bathe, brush their teeth and use the bathroom every day. We see these activities as essential to maintaining life. Many, however, claim that they would like to exercise but they just can't find the time. But if one regards exercise as a truly essential activity (like taking a shower before going to a job interview), the time can be readily found.

You wouldn't put off showering for one week because you had an especially busy week at work. After a couple of days you'd surely start feeling and looking pretty yucky and smelling considerably worse. People who view exercise as indispensable to their lives feel uncomfortable in much the same way if they don't exercise for a few days in a row.

The truth is that we always find the time to do what is extremely important or urgent. Most people would agree that exercising is important. The problem is that they don't necessarily see it as an urgent problem that needs to be dealt with immediately. Therefore, it gets set aside in order to complete other tasks that may need more immediate attention although they may be a lot less important in the long run.

For animals living in their natural habitat there is virtually no obesity. Pets and animals kept in captivity are at risk of becoming overweight but those in the wild just don't get fat.

Consider the example of a cheetah hanging out in the Serengeti. When the cheetah is hungry and she spots an antelope she'll likely chase the beast down to try to procure herself a meal. Sometimes she'll succeed in capturing dinner, sometimes she won't. In either case she'll have expended an awful lot of calories during her effort.

When she is able to nab the prey, she most definitely will not immediately go for seconds. She still has to rest to recover from the effort she put out for the first kill. Cheetahs don't overeat. Moreover, every time they want to eat they have to run. Exercise is naturally built into their regular daily activities.

Compare that with a typical office worker who sits behind a desk all day typing on a computer keyboard as a way to obtain his food. With the money he earns, despite the minimal consumption of calories, he can go to any drive-through window of a fast-food restaurant and procure himself a meal without even getting out of the car. Furthermore, he can obtain two hamburgers with about the same effort that it takes to order one. One can easily feed oneself without ever getting out of a chair.

Of course I'm not suggesting that everyone should get in the habit of hunting down one's lunch or change their career in order to start working in a coal mine. The conveniences of the lifestyle many of us are able to enjoy are absolutely wonderful. They allow us to spend more time with our families, in leisure, or being more productive in other ventures. However, due to the comforts that our lifestyle affords us, exercise becomes an absolute necessity in order to maintain health and avoid obesity. Cheetahs don't need to go to the gym to work out. Humans do.

Most people, when asked how to deal with weight management or weight loss, instantly respond by mentioning diet. That's probably why so many are frustrated by their inability to effectively lose or keep off weight for the long term. Diets alone simply do not work for the vast majority of people, and should not be considered the central part of a weight loss plan. Exercise, on the other hand, is the cornerstone to weight management.

In the short term (over several weeks) one can lose weight by simply restricting the number of calories consumed. The problem is that denying your body the pleasure of food is extremely uncomfortable. At the end of World War II, as a result of witnessing the horrors of the holocaust, some scientific studies on starvation were performed on volunteers. The subjects of the study were given a diet that resulted in weight loss. One of the findings of the study was that as the individuals continued to lose weight, their thoughts began to increasingly revolve around food. Soon, all they could think about was food! Their mood also changed to apathy and depression.

It is no wonder that inevitably, someone who is at first successfully losing weight while on a restrictive diet will return to eating at his pre-diet level. Restricting your food intake to such a degree that you are losing weight cannot be sustained indefinitely. What many people don't realize is that as soon as you stop dieting you will quickly regain the weight back and usually end up at a slightly higher weight than before the diet. As a result, many people are frustrated with trying to lose weight to the point that they may give up all together. Some patients tell me "Doctor, we've tried everything. Nothing works." In reality they've tried only all the wrong things.

When you restrict your intake of calories by dieting, your body does everything possible to economize the number of calories it burns. The body assumes that there is a lack of accessibility to food. Therefore, the basal metabolic rate goes down. Your body is trying to save energy just as I might turn off the lights and reset the thermostat on my air conditioner if my electric bills are too high. It is a wonderful, protective mechanism if in fact you are in a period of famine.

The problem is that when you interrupt the diet, your body continues to work at the more efficient set point for a while until the basal metabolic rate returns to the pre-diet level. That's why many people gain all the weight back (and usually more) at the end of a diet.

The other problem with extreme dieting is that you not only are burning fat, but in fact are also losing lean body mass such as muscle. Since even at rest, muscle tissue burns more calories than fat tissue, the last thing you want to do is get rid of muscle mass. In children, the idea of losing muscle weight by restricting caloric intake is particularly frightening.

In summary, diets result in a reduction of basal metabolic rate, a loss of lean body mass (which further reduces the number of calories burned at rest), and cannot be sustained indefinitely because of the deep sense of discomfort and dissatisfaction that it creates for the individual. Diets don't work. Anyone trying to manage his weight would do well by eating a well-balanced diet, relatively high in fiber and low in fat as detailed in the "food pyramid" diagram of the American Dietetic Association.

Exercise produces the exact opposite results of dieting. Almost everyone is aware that exercising burns calories during the actual exercise period. What they may be unaware of is that even at the completion of the exercise session, the body continues to burn calories at a slightly higher rate. Of course one of the benefits of exercise is that it builds lean body mass by increasing the bulk of muscles. As a consequence, you continue to burn calories at a higher rate even at rest.

Finally, rather than producing a feeling of apathy or depression, exercise tends to produce a general sense of wellbeing. This is commonly known as the "runner's high" and is believed to be due to the release of certain chemical messengers which stimulate your brain to produce this general sense of pleasure. It is no surprise, therefore, that many people are able to stick with an exercise program, not just for days or a couple of weeks, but for their entire lives. It becomes a pleasurable habit.

This, of course is what we must expect our children to do. Our goal must be that they continue to exercise not only through their teenage years, but into their twenties, forties, seventies and hopefully beyond. I have an aunt in her mid-eighties who still exercises daily (she goes swimming at the beach every day throughout the summer), and is in excellent cardiovascular shape. She is fast becoming somewhat of a living legend in her city.

Weight management is just one facet of health management. It requires a sustained, life-long commitment. Get thin quick programs are about as effective as get rich quick schemes, though the latter are more likely to land you in jail. If you are planning to have some money set aside for retirement, the best plan is to consistently save a small portion of your earnings throughout your working career, hopefully in some sort of account which pays you an interest rate that outpaces inflation. Playing the lottery on every other payday or planning a weekend in Las Vegas on your sixty-fifth birthday is what financial planners describe as "poor financial planning".

Likewise, jumping into a crash diet for one month to shed a few pounds is no substitute for a lifetime of moderate exercise. There is no way to avoid the fact that exercise is essential.

How do we get our children to exercise? Of course we must serve as an example. You cannot expect a child to exercise if the last time you broke a sweat was back in high school when you had to run two whole laps around the football field (and be honest, you ended up walking the last lap). A regular exercise routine would be mandatory for any parent or adult planning to have a baby if, through a curious series of political events, I were suddenly elected benevolent tyrant of this country (I have a lot of other good ideas too).

Furthermore, it is important to select a form of exercise that your child, and hopefully the entire family, finds enjoyable. If the only form of exercise I could choose from was swimming laps or riding a stationary bicycle I would soon give up exercising altogether. Luckily, I really look forward to playing soccer, and basketball's not too bad either. My wife on the other hand, loves to swim back and forth in a swimming pool. The key is to find something you and your child can enjoy.

A word of warning: little league baseball does not provide enough of an aerobic workout. It can be very enjoyable, a worthwhile social experience for your child, and can help improve his coordination. For my son, little league was crucial in developing his interest in entomology. Unfortunately, his field studies of insects were interrupted every so often by the occasional annoying ball that somehow managed to roll over into the outfield. By itself, little league baseball should not be considered sufficient exercise for your child.

Sports that require sustained activity are probably the most effective choice for keeping children fit. For children under the age of five, though, most team sports are not appropriate. It is crucial for parents of younger children to actively participate in physical activity with their sons and daughters.

Some children are just not interested in sports. For children (and adults) who are not athletically inclined the best exercise is walking at a brisk pace. For a person who is not in good physical condition, a fifteen-minute walk four times a week is a good start. Gradually, the walk should be increased to thirty minutes, every other day.

The key is that the walk should proceed at a brisk pace. Window- shopping at the mall is not what I have in mind. Nor is walking to and from school, although I would encourage this if it is a safe option. The point is that there should be a designated exercise time where the activity performed is for the sole purpose of exercising. We want our children to learn that exercise is a necessary routine. My definition of exercise is physical activity that is performed for the sole purpose of improving one's health.

In order to encourage children to exercise I suggest having special exercise clothes which should include comfortable sneakers. The exercise session should start with some gentle stretching. You should walk at a rate faster than your usual walking-through-the shopping mall pace, but not so fast that it will lead to exhaustion within five minutes. You're doing well if during the activity your heart is beating faster, your breathing is a little deeper and faster even though you may not be actually sweating. Upon termination of the activity you should again stretch out, or continue to walk at a slow pace.

It is important to realize that for most people moderate exercise is probably better than intense exercise because of the lower risk of injury. Of course, there are some people who think they can maximize their exercise session by wearing layers of sweatshirts while jogging in ninety-degree weather. Doctors have a scientific term to refer to this type of individual. The term is "idiot".

Your clothing should not in any way hamper your body's ability to radiate the extra heat that it is producing. Let me remind you that the ultimate goal of exercise is improved health. Heat stroke is not healthy.

Chapter 8

M = Motivate Your Child with Rewards

In order to help your child acquire new habits or change old habits, you must be able to exert some influence on your child's behavior. Ultimately, we are only able to have complete control over our own behavior. We cannot control others, even through hypnosis. Nevertheless, we are sometimes able to alter the probability that another person will perform a certain deed, especially if we have a significant relationship with that person. Animal trainers are very adept at using techniques that psychologists refer to as "behavior modification" or "operant conditioning", which were in large part developed by B. F. Skinner. I will try to give some advice on interacting with your children.

Our brains are very good at forming and analyzing associations. Let's say for example that we are exposed to a whistling sound, which is followed a few seconds later by a very loud blasting sound. If we are exposed repeatedly to the sequence of the whistle followed by the blast, soon we will come to expect and predict the blast as soon as we hear the whistle. An association is formed between the whistle and the loud blast.

In a similar fashion we form associations throughout our lifetime. Some of these associations serve us well, whereas others may deceive us. Let's say I try eating sushi for the first time in my life, and the next morning I awaken with a terrible stomachache and vomiting. I am likely to associate the illness with eating sushi. I may never eat sushi again. However, it may have just been a coincidence that I got sick that morning and had nothing to do with the raw fish I forked out so much money for just to please my wife. Or perhaps that was really bad sushi, whereas other sushi is just fine and not likely to make me sick.

As I am kneeling, doubled over in pain next to the toilet, I am forming an association between sushi and feeling sick. The strength of this association may change with time or with other experiences. Let's say I try eating sushi again. If I get sick again that association will become stronger and I will not likely eat in a Japanese restaurant for the rest of my life. But if I don't get sick the next five times I eat sushi, the association will progressively weaken, and I'll be more likely to continue spending my money on raw fish.

When we perform an act, we frequently receive some form of feedback or response. This feedback may be quite subtle, like a smile from a passerby when we say "Good morning", or it can be dramatic, such as a standing ovation after we sing the national anthem in front of 50,000 spectators before a football game. This feedback affects the probability that we will perform that particular act again in the future.

When the response we get is pleasant or gratifying, it increases the likelihood that we will repeat that behavior. This is called positive reinforcement. When the response is painful or distressing, it lowers the probability that we will repeat that deed. This is called negative reinforcement. A simplistic but useful way to think of this is to think of positive reinforcement as a reward, whereas negative reinforcement can be translated as punishment. Again, this is overly simplistic because sometimes when we suffer as a result of our actions it is not because we are being punished by anyone. We are just facing the consequences of our poor decisions.

In general, positive reinforcement is more effective in altering behavior than negative reinforcement. Moreover, focusing on rewarding desirable behavior rather than punishing undesirable behavior tends to be a more humane approach and will strengthen the relationship between parent and child rather than compromise it.

Negative reinforcement is only effective if the negative response immediately follows the behavior and occurs consistently every time that behavior is performed. Cancer is feared and dreaded by most. One would imagine that it would be an effective negative reinforcer, yet for millions of smokers the fear of cancer does not reduce or eliminate the behavior of smoking. That's because it does not have the characteristics needed for effective negative reinforcement.

First of all, not all smokers get cancer. In order for negative reinforcement to be effective in reducing a behavior, the negative consequence has to follow 100% of the time, or at the very least the individual must perceive that the ill effect will always follow. Second, when cancer does develop, it is not immediately subsequent to the behavior. In fact, it usually appears decades after the behavior has become entrenched as a habit.

A much more effective (though ethically dubious) negative reinforcement system in achieving smoking cessation (at least for males), would be an immediate, swift kick in the groin. Just imagine if, as soon as a man took one puff from a cigarette he were immediately kicked in the groin. This would happen every time he lit up, no matter where he was. The association of smoking with intense throbbing pain in the genitals would be quickly formed because the feedback would be immediate. The man would soon appreciate that the pain would inevitably result every single time he lit up. Most men would give up smoking within 24 hours. Of course, if three months later he lit up again, he would need to be kicked in the groin to avoid re-establishing the habit.

As effective as such a system would be, it would be highly impractical to put into effect. After all, someone would need to spy on the subject 24 hours a day, ready to kick him in the groin. That's the problem with relying on negative reinforcement in altering people's behavior. Often what happens is that the subject becomes more efficient at lying and covering up the undesired behavior in order to avoid the negative repercussions rather than change his behavior.

In trying to establish healthy habits in our children, we want the experience to be enjoyable. We want the process to enrich our relationship with our sons and daughters, not destroy it. That is why I encourage the use of positive reinforcement in this program.

Some parents frown on the idea of using behavior modification techniques altogether. Their reasoning is that their children are not animals which need to be trained, or marionettes we can manipulate. I want to be clear that I do not suggest that we should be puppeteers and deny our children their individuality. I am only proposing that as parents we have more life experience, and therefore better judgement than our children do. We clearly have a responsibility to educate our children about which behaviors are likely to serve them best in life.

Whether we are conscious of it or not, our children are constantly getting feedback from us. Too often, the feedback is inconsistent or contradictory and may actually reinforce behaviors we are trying to discourage. That is why all parents should be aware of behavior modification techniques, not to manipulate, but to educate.

But isn't giving rewards for a behavior essentially a form of bribery? There is a distinct difference between bribes and rewards. In the former, one is coerced into performing a certain behavior (which would otherwise not occur) with the promise of compensation. In the latter, one is being compensated or complimented for a deed he has already completed. When we use rewards we are only increasing the probability that the behavior will happen again.

The most effective way to utilize positive reinforcement to encourage a behavior is to establish a "token economy". A good example of a token economy can be witnessed by visiting one of many popular pizza and game parlor chains. When children play the electronic games they are rewarded, not only with the enjoyment of playing the game, but by receiving some tickets. Typically, the better you perform in the game the more tickets you get.

At the end of the evening, the tickets can be traded in for a toy. No matter that 100 tickets will get you a cheap plastic toy worth about 25 cents. The sight of the tickets as they are being dispensed from the machines is a powerful positive reinforcement, not only for the children but for the parents as well. It gives the child a sense of accomplishment and self-worth that all children crave.

Token economies have been successfully used in schools as well as jails (where cigarettes are usually utilized), but the ultimate token economy is money. Not many people wish they had less money.

Money is a positive reinforcer even though there is not much practical use for a small rectangular piece of paper stamped with black and green ink. Of course the money can be traded in for a variety of toys of your choice, just like the tickets at the pizza parlor.

An employer could decide to compensate an employee by giving him a muffler one week, four hubcaps the next and so on, until after eight months the employee will have an entire car. Most employees would opt for money instead. Likewise, the promise of buying a toy next weekend is not as effective as the immediate dispensing of tickets or points that the child can then trade in for that toy (for example, 20 tickets could be worth $1 at the toy store).

It is important to realize that many of the motivating forces which drive children's behavior are identical to those of adults. Some of the strongest are the desire to feel important, the need to belong, and the desire for affection. Positive reinforcement fulfills many, if not all these needs, if we do it without coercion. By helping our children feel important and loved we strengthen the ties between us and make it more likely that our children will continue to show interest in the activities we are encouraging them to undertake.

Let's see how a token economy with positive reinforcement can be used to encourage a behavior in a child. First you explain the nature of the token economy. You need to explain that you will start giving the child some tickets or points that he can ultimately trade in for purchases at a toy store (for younger kids) or clothing store (older kids). You must explain exactly what each ticket is worth. For example, 20 tickets could have the value of $1. The child may cash in the tickets at any time she wants and will have opportunities to earn more tickets even after she cashes the tickets in. This way she has the option of buying relatively inexpensive toys, or of saving up the tickets to purchase something of greater value.

One of the great things about using a token economy is that you are not only rewarding your child for desirable behavior, you are also teaching him the value of earning and saving. At my house, our children earn all their goodies except at Christmas and birthdays.

You need not necessarily tell your child what it is you are going to reward – he will find out soon enough – but you can if you wish. The key to behavior modification is good planning. You must decide exactly what behaviors you want to encourage and then work on one behavior at a time. This is crucial. Pick only one behavior to work on at a time. When you have managed good progress with that behavior you can move on to another one.

If you want to improve your basketball game you should work first on your dribble, then on your shooting, then on your rebounding skills. The order you do this in is not critical but it is important to work on one skill at a time. That's the idea behind practice drills.

Once you've decided what behavior your child would like to do, start rewarding your child for even the slightest effort toward that behavior. Be generous at first. Then become slowly more selective in delivering the reward so that your child is gradually approaching the behavior you are trying to elicit. If you're trying to encourage your child to exercise, at first you would reward him just for putting on his sneakers and going outside. After he does this a couple of times, you would get more selective and wait for him to walk five minutes before rewarding him. Gradually you would expect slightly more effort until eventually you are rewarding him only after he has walked at a brisk pace for 25 minutes.

Try to break down each behavior into many little steps rather than trying to tackle it as a single act. The process is one of many little successes leading toward the final complete act. You do not want to reward only the final complete behavior. Let you child enjoy each little triumph as he is gradually approaching the behavior you are striving for. Avoid the temptation to criticize or coerce your child if he doesn't complete a step. Have patience. Perhaps back up a step so that you can reward him again.

What if we are not trying to encourage a new act but are trying to get rid of an old habit? This tends to be more challenging because it requires more creativity, and it's easier to develop new habits than getting rid of old ones. The ways to get rid of an old habit is by either changing the environment in such a way that the habit can no longer continue, or to introduce a new behavior that is inconsistent with the old habit.

Let's look at some examples of changing the environment to get rid of an undesired behavior. Someone with a drinking problem could move to Saudi Arabia where he has no access to liquor. A cat which is constantly tearing up the sofa with its nails can be made an outdoors cat. If a toddler keeps drinking from a baby bottle, all the baby bottles can be thrown in the trash. If a child is addicted to the television set, the TV can be packed in a box and placed in the attic, or donated to the Salvation Army. All these examples involve removing the opportunity for the continued behavior.

Sometimes this approach requires rather drastic measures, but in cases where the behavior would predictably happen if the opportunity remains, this may be the easiest and most effective way of stopping the behavior. For children who are unable to unglue themselves from the television, getting rid of all the TV sets is not such an unreasonable maneuver.

There is another option, however, which involves introducing a new habit which is inconsistent with the old one. Let's take the example of a child who watches too much television. You would want to reward a behavior which is impossible to accomplish while watching TV. In fact you could reward more than one behavior, all of which are inconsistent with television viewing.

You might reward reading a book, riding a bike, or drawing pictures so that the probability of these desired behaviors happening again in the future increases. As I mentioned in the chapter on limiting the amount of time children spend watching television, it is not enough to tell your child to stop watching so much TV. You must present options and make those options even more pleasurable than watching TV, perhaps with the aid of direct positive reinforcement.

The basic principles of behavior modification are rather simple, but to use them effectively takes a little practice and patience because of most people's natural tendency to resort to scolding, nagging, coercing and criticizing. There are excellent books that deal exclusively with this subject which you may read if you are having difficulty obtaining results with this technique. My aim was to provide the basic tools rather than providing a detailed analysis of behavior modification. In most cases this knowledge will be sufficient in achieving the desired goals.

Chapter 9

D = Dine Restaurant Style, Not Buffet Style

When you eat in a restaurant, the waiter serves you items that you selected from a menu. If you finish your portion, you don't get seconds unless you agree to pay for another entrée. The portions are predetermined by the chef and placed on a plate in the kitchen.

At an all-you-can-eat buffet, however, if you enjoyed the fried chicken you can always go back for a few more pieces, and while you're there you might as well get some more potato salad. After all, unless you are stuffed to the gills you don't really feel like you got your money's worth. Buffet style eating encourages overeating.

Not only should you avoid getting in the habit of frequenting buffets when you dine out, you must avoid eating buffet style at home. If you prepare the dinner table by having a large bowl of fried chicken as a centerpiece, and various other bowls of mashed potatoes and green beans from which everyone can serve themselves without having to get up, you are eating buffet style.

If those mashed potatoes taste pretty good and there's a large bowl just within arm's reach, it is too easy to go for seconds. If on the other hand, it is understood from the outset that the portions have already been determined, and just like in a restaurant you should not expect seconds, the likelihood of overeating is diminished.

Get into the habit of eating restaurant style. Serve what you believe is an appropriate portion on a dish while still in the kitchen. It shouldn't be a tiny portion, just a regular appropriate portion on a normal sized plate. If after eating the serving a family member is still hungry, have him or her wait until everyone else has finished their serving. By this I don't mean that everyone else has to finish every last crumb on his plate. No one should be forced to continue eating after they no longer feel hungry. Everyone else is finished eating when they no longer feel like eating what is on their plate. Then bring out a bowl of salad (it is better to eat salad after a meal rather than before the main meal), or fresh fruit.

The reason for the delay until everyone else has finished eating is what I refer to as the fifteen-minute rule. This is a phenomenon that I unofficially discovered with a couple of my classmates while in medical school. We were all very poor as we pursued our education, and could easily eat more than we could readily afford. In order to get by, we resorted to joining as many student organizations on campus as possible because they always served food at their meetings. We attended meetings of PSR (Physicians for Social Responsibility), Amnesty International, and went to all the student government meetings (they always served poor boy sandwiches, and there was usually enough to take some home. That worked pretty well in the first two years of medical school, but we just didn't have enough time to go to these meetings during the third and fourth years. Luckily, that's when we discovered the fifteen-minute rule. Essentially, the principle is that when you are hungry, it takes at least fifteen minutes for the sensation of hunger to dissipate after you have eaten. If you eat real fast and finish all your food in five minutes you will still be hungry. You'll easily be able to eat more. But if you wait fifteen minutes, you may find that you now feel satiated. While you're eating, you're stomach is producing gastric juices and your salivary glands continue secreting saliva. It takes a little while for all this machinery to slow down to a stop.

People who eat fast tend to eat more. In some situations, as long as you keep eating, you can keep on eating. This usually happens on holidays, where people can eat non-stop for a couple of hours, and don't realize just how full they are until they shuffle over to the sofa. It is important to understand that there may be a lag between the last bite of a meal and the disappearance of the sensation of hunger.

It is helpful to try to slow down the speed at which your child consumes a meal. There are a couple of strategies to accomplish this. You can have your child place his fork on the table between bites, and have him wait until he has fully chewed and swallowed that mouthful before picking up the fork again. The second, and perhaps more effective method is to have your child take a sip from a large glass of water after every two mouthfuls. Another good idea is to avoid having your child eat alone where he might shovel food into his mouth as fast as he can. Make dinner time a social event for the family where everyone can contribute to the conversation.

These mealtime habits all have the purpose of limiting overeating, rather than denying normal sized portions. Also, I don't feel strongly about eliminating any specific foods from the dinner table (unlike my approach to between-meal snacks) as long as one eats each item in moderation. For the most part, parents tend to prepare nutritionally sound foods though the portions may be too large. One should be able to enjoy a meal because of the quality of the food and the company, rather than the quantity of food served.

Chapter 10

O = Offer Fewer, Better Snacks

I like to think that in the majority of families, when children sit down to eat meals prepared by their caretakers, they are served a variety of nutritious foods including rice, pasta, beans, fruits, vegetables and lean meats. For many children, the problem does not lie with what they eat at breakfast, lunch and dinner, but with what they eat between meals. Common snacks include potato chips (and a variety of deep-fried chips which do not seem to be made out of potatoes), candy bars, and soda.

These snacks tend to contain lots of salt, sugar, and fat. They don't contribute anything worthwhile in terms of nutrition, and when eaten on a regular basis, can add a huge number of calories to a person's diet. These excessive calories are unfortunately not transformed into muscle or brain tissue, but fat. Some overweight children engage in an eating pattern that has been described as "grazing". Essentially, it consists of snacking at a rather constant rate throughout the waking hours of the day. Grazing is a form of feeding appropriate for large herbivores such as cows and elephants, but when adopted by children, it inevitably results in obesity.

For these reasons, I routinely counsel parents of children who need to reduce their caloric intake to focus first on curbing snacks rather than sharply cutting back on regular meals. It is useful to remember that about 3,500 calories are roughly equivalent to one pound of body fat. Let's take the example of a child who enjoys eating a popular deep-fried corn meal snack. Although a ten ounce bag is considered by the manufacturer to contain 10 servings (1 serving = 21 pieces), he can easily eat half a bag in one sitting. Let's assume that he is able to exert self-control and eat only one serving. He would take in 160 Calories, 90 of which are from fat. Of course since this particular snack has 290 mg of sodium, the child gets thirsty and decides to drink an 8 fluid ounce serving of Coca-Cola that contains 140 calories per serving. The total now is 300 calories.

Now let's assume that he eats this type of snack only three times a week. In one year's time the number of calories coming just from this thrice weekly snack habit would total 46,800, which is equivalent to just over thirteen pounds of body fat. To burn off this number of calories by exercising would require about 85 hours of jogging at 11 miles per hour. Two things become apparent from this example. First, small changes in caloric intake carried on for long periods of time can result in large fluctuations in weight. Second, a large amount of exercise is required to burn off the extra calories taken in from snacks (about an hour of exercise for each snack in our example, depending on the type of exercise chosen).

If an individual engages in extra exercise to burn off the additional calories taken in from snacking, he remains in net balance. But if he does not, he starts accumulating a calorie debt. Just like a credit card, over time the debt gets harder and harder to pay off. If one is making only the minimum payments due on his credit card but continues spending at the same rate, the credit card debt will never be paid off; in fact it will continue to grow. If a child starts a moderately intense exercise program but continues to eat high calorie snacks between regular meals, he will continue to gain weight. The exercise is necessary, but must be accompanied by a reduction in caloric intake.

Some toddlers can be given excessive calories in the form of milk or juice. A child over one year of age should not drink more than 16 ounces of milk a day. By this time, a child should be receiving most of his calories from foods rather than milk. Please note that the American Academy of Pediatrics recommends that in the first year of life infants be fed breast milk or formula. Cow's milk should not be introduced until after the first birthday in order to minimize the risk of iron deficiency anemia and cow's milk allergies. Between 1 and 2 years of age, children should be given whole milk. Low- fat milk such as skim milk or 2% milk fat should not be given until after the second birthday due to the higher fat requirements of children of this age to aid in the development of the brain.

Likewise, the quantity of juice should be kept at below about 12 ounces per day. This applies not just to children over one year of age (as is the case with milk), but to children of any age. Children who drink excessive amounts of milk and juice are typically still taking the bottle. Pediatricians strongly urge discontinuing the use of the bottle after the first birthday for a variety of medical reasons. Prolonged use of the bottle can lead to a severe form of tooth decay and orthodontic problems. Drinking from a bottle while lying down has been shown to contribute to ear- infections, one of the most common reasons for visits to pediatricians. Picky eaters tend to eat worse if they take large amounts of milk and juice, whereas overeaters take additional calories they don't need by continuing the baby bottle habit.

In terms of limiting snacks I have several suggestions. First of all, don't buy and keep junk food like potato chips, candy, and chocolate bars in the house. Remove the temptation altogether. If an alcoholic relative were to come visit you for a few days, you wouldn't want to have beer, wine, scotch whiskey and other liquors readily available all over the house. It is easier to not have potato chips in the home than to reason (or argue) with your child to not eat them. If your children insist that you buy a lot of junk every time you go grocery shopping, find a way to go shopping without the kids. Unless your child has the ability to buy his own food, the supplier of junk food is typically the parent.

If your child receives an allowance and inevitably spends the money on junk food, do not pay the allowance in cash, but rather deposit it into a savings account, from which he can draw money to buy goods other than junk food under your supervision. You would not give money to a child if you knew he would use it to buy drugs. Likewise, you should not subsidize your child's unhealthy junk food habit.

Set a house rule whereby the children are not allowed to help themselves to food in the pantry or refrigerator without permission. If they are hungry, they should inform you rather than make the decision of what to eat and when to eat it without supervision.

In the event that they are too hungry to wait another couple of hours for lunch or dinner, prepare a snack consisting of fruit or raw vegetables, such as celery or baby carrots. The advantage of this type of snack is that it is nutritious, low in calories, and has no fat. Of course you don't want to ruin it by putting a thick layer of peanut butter over an apple slice, or by dipping pieces of celery in a thick, high-fat, high-calorie dip.

If your child is watching television when he gets hungry and asks for a snack, make him choose one of two options: turn the TV off and sit at the dinner table to eat the snack, or wait until the show is over and then sit at the table to eat the snack. There can be no snacking in front of the TV. Having options, even when limited, allows the child to feel in control of her behavior, rather than manipulated by her parents.

Eating snacks should not become a daily ritual. It should not be considered a hobby or a pastime. It should be an unusual occurrence that occurs for one reason only: to satisfy a truly uncomfortable sensation of hunger that cannot wait until the next meal with the entire family.

Chapter 11

W = When in Doubt, Walk

In many countries, people can get a workout just going about their regular business. They walk or ride their bikes to school and work. They walk to the grocery store and carry back several bags of food. They wash dishes by hand.

In most communities in the United States this may not be practical or safe. The nearest grocery store may be four miles away. There might not be a sidewalk on the highway that leads to school, making walking a real hazard. Most new communities are being built with the driver rather than the pedestrian in mind.

Nonetheless, we can try to maximize our energy expenditure and that of our children while going about our daily activities, if we make a conscious effort. When possible, walking to work and to the store provides the opportunity to burn a few calories and improve our physical fitness.

I must confess I have a natural tendency to seek out and conquer the parking space closest to the door whenever I go to the store, the bank, or the post office. This is second nature for most people. It takes a conscious effort on my part to park farther away, perhaps at the edge of the parking lot, and walk the extra few yards. This is a useful tactic, not only to help with fitness, but also to avoid dents and scratches on your car since there is usually much more space there.

When inside a building or a shopping mall, it's a good idea to avoid routinely using elevators and escalators. If you need to go up one or two stories, take the stairs. Going down is easier, so it's reasonable to take the stairs for even four or five stories. Get your children in the habit of doing the same.

Some studies have shown that people who tend not to become overweight are more fidgety than individuals who are obese. Even when sitting down at a desk, the slim individuals are burning more calories just by tapping their fingers or their feet. One way to try to get to move more, even when you're doing nothing, is to squeeze a compressible rubber ball or one of those squishy "stress-relievers". Your child could get in the habit of doing this while watching television or while riding in the car.

When grocery shopping, avoid having your child ride in the basket. Let him walk. Have him help you load and unload the car. If there are only a couple of bags to carry, avoid using the basket to wheel the groceries to the car. If you're carrying plastic bags with handles you could even do some biceps flexes while you're walking.

A form of exercise that many people underestimate is housework. Mopping the floor for thirty minutes burns about 120 calories, which is close to the 135 calories you could burn by riding a bicycle at approximately 5.5 miles per hour during that amount of time. Having your child help with some household chores can improve his fitness, teach him some responsibility, and slightly reduce the amount of work left to you.

Reasonable chores include making the bed, carrying laundry to the washer, helping to fold the laundry, setting and clearing the dinner table, and helping to wash the car. These chores are more fun if done in someone's company, especially if you play some lively dance music to get you in the mood.

Our society has been extremely effective in reducing the effort involved in many daily activities. In fact, our life can be so effortless that we need to actually seek out ways to use more energy and effort in order to maintain fitness. Help your child see that doing things the hard way can sometimes be more fun. When I'm older, I doubt I will remember exactly what it was like to drive my children to school while living in Texas-unfortunately, the school is five miles away from our house. But walking the three blocks to their school in Illinois on a cool autumn morning, with leaves of every color creating a painter's palette on the sidewalks will be etched in my memory forever.

Chapter 12

N = Never Talk the Talk if you Can't Walk the Walk

Children tend to model their behavior on the people who are around them on a daily basis. In the first decade of life parents are undoubtedly the strongest influence on a child's life. In the teenage years children yearn to fit in with their peers, but if a solid relationship is created and maintained, the child will continue to strive to meet a parent's expectations.

Of course, it is important that children receive very clear messages from their parents. If a father lights up a cigarette but turns to his son to say, "Boy, I hope you never start smoking. It's a terrible habit" the child is receiving a very confusing message. If you don't want your child to smoke, don't smoke. If you want your child to buckle his seatbelt in the car, always buckle up before starting the engine. If you want your child to have religion in his life, go to church and have religion in your life. If you want your child to exercise, let him see you exercise.

As the saying goes, if you want to talk the talk, you've got to walk the walk. Preferably, do more walking than talking. If your child sees you exercise, that picture is more vivid and more memorable than any speech you give him on the importance of exercise. In many ways this last recommendation in the SLIM DOWN program is the first one that should be adopted. To try to encourage your child to incorporate habits that are not part of his parent's life is not a reasonable or fair expectation.

There are plenty of reasons for adults to exercise regularly, avoid a sedentary lifestyle and avoid overeating, mainly to improve health and maintain fitness. For an adult who is also a parent, the most significant and deeply profound motivation should be to instill these habits in his children. To ensure our children's continued health and wellbeing is one of our most important responsibilities as parents, surpassing the responsibility to provide for the child in materialistic terms.

Be a role model for your child. Try to appreciate the enormity of this task. Try to understand what an honor it is to be in your position. Most importantly, live your life the way you hope your child will live his.

For further reading

Andersen RE et al. Relationship of physical activity and television watching with body weight and level of fatness among children: results from the Third National Health and Nutrition Examination Survey. JAMA: 1998; 279: 938-42.

Bandini LG and Dietz WH. Myths about childhood obesity. Pediatric Annals: 1992; 21: 647-52.

Berenson G et al. Obesity and cardiovascular risk in children. Annals New York Academy of Sciences;1993: 93-102.

Birch L and Fisher J. Appetite and eating behavior in children. Pediatric Clinics of North America: 1995; 42: 931-953.

Boschert S. Top nutritional problem in kids is now obesity. Pediatric News: December 1996; 29.

Carek P et al. Management of obesity: medical treatment options. American Family Physician: 1997; 55: 551-558.

Dietz WH and Robinson TN. Assessment and treatment of childhood obesity. Pediatrics in Review: 1993; 14; 337-43.

Dietz WH. Therapeutic strategies in childhood obesity. Hormone Research: 1993; 39: 86-90.

Epstein L et al. Decreasing sedentary behaviors in treating pediatric obesity. Arch Pediatr Adolesc Med: 2000; 154: 220-226.

Epstein LH et al. Exercise in treating obesity in children and adolescents. Medicine and Science in Sports and Exercise: 1996; 28: 428-35.

Epstein LH. Exercise in the treatment of childhood obesity. International Journal of Obesity and Related Metaboic Disorders: 1995; 4: S117-21.

Figueroa-Colon R et al. Prevalence of obesity with increased blood pressure in elemenatary school-aged children. South Med J: 1997; 90: 806-813.

Gortmaker SL et al. Television viewing as a cause of increasing obesity among children in the United States. Arch Peds and Adolescent Med: 1996; 150: 356-362.

Gutin B. Physical Activity in the prevention of childhood obesity. Annals New York Academy of Sciences: 1993; 115-125.

Harlan W. Epidemiology of childhood obesity. Annals New York Academy of Sciences: 699; 1993:1-4.

Kaufer Christoffel K and Ariza A. The epidemiology of overweight in children: relevance for clinical care. Pediatrics: 1998; 101: 103-105.

Kumanyika S. Ethnicity and obesity development in children. Annals New York Academy of Sciences: 1993; 81-90.

Must A. Morbidity and mortality associated with elevated body weight in children and adolescents. American Journal of Clinical Nutrition: 1996; 63: 445-447.

Parizkova J. Obesity and its treatment by diet and exercise. World Review of Nutrition and Dietetics: 1993; 72: 78-91.

Rees J. A comprehensive protocol for assessment of obese adolescents and evaluation of their progress in managing weight. Annals New York Academy of Sciences: 1993; 280-285.

Roberts S. Early diet and obesity. Carnation Nutrition Education Series; 2: 303-316.

Robinson TN. Reducing children's television viewing to prevent obesity: a randomized controlled study. JAMA: 1999; 282: 1561.

Rocchini A. Adolescent obesity and hypertension. Pediatric Clinics of North America: 1993: 40: 81-91.

Roche A. Methodological considerations in the assessment of obesity. Annals New York Academy of Sciences: 1993: 6-17.

Schonfeld-Warden N and Warden C. Pediatric obesity: an overview of etiology and treatment. Pediatric Clinics of North America: 1997; 44: 339-361.

Serdula MK et al. Do obese children become obese adults? A review of the literature. Preventive Medicine: 1993; 22: 167-77.

Sondike S et al. Bringing a formidable opponent down to size. Contemporary Pediatrics: 2000; 17: 133-157.

Sothern MS et al. An effective multidisciplinary approach to weight reduction in youth. Annals New York Academy of Sciences: 1993; 292-293.

Suskind RM et al. Recent advances in the treatment of childhood obesity. Annals New York Academy of Sciences: 1993; 181-197.

Troiano RP et al. Overweight prevalence and trends for children and adolescents: the National Health and Nutrition Examination Surveys, 1963-1991. Arch Pediatr Adolesc Med: 1995; 149: 1085-91.

Wallace W et al. Obesity in children: A risk for depression. Annals New York Academy of Sciences: 1993; 301-303.

Whitaker R et al. Predicting obesity in young adulthood from childhood and parental obesity. New Engl J Med: 1997; 337: 869-873.

Williams C. Treatment of childhood obesity in pediatric practice. Annals New York Academy of Sciences: 1993; 207-219.

Printed in the United States
1010500002B

9 781581 127447